Lives and Times

Helen Keller

Emma Lynch

Heinemann Library
Chicago, Illinois

Designed by Richard Parker and Tinstar Design Ltd
(www.tinstar.co.uk)
Originated by Repro Multi Warna
Printed and bound in China by South China Printing Company

09 08 07 06 05
10 9 8 7 6 5 4 3 2 1

Library of Congress Cataloging-in-Publication Data
Lynch, Emma.
    Helen Keller / Emma Lynch.
        p. cm. -- (Lives and times)
    Includes bibliographical references and index.
    ISBN 1-4034-6350-6 (lib. bdg. : alk. paper) -- ISBN 1-4034-6364-6 (pbk. : alk. paper) 1. Keller, Helen, 1880-1968--Juvenile literature. 2. Blind-deaf women--United States--Biography--Juvenile literature. 3. Sullivan, Annie, 1866-1936--Juvenile literature. I. Title. II. Series: Lives and times (Des Plaines, Ill.)
    HV1624.K4L95 2005
    362.4'1'092--dc22
                            2004018007

Acknowledgments
The author and Publisher are grateful to the following for permission to reproduce copyright material: pp. 4, 14, 18, 19 Corbis/Bettmann; pp. 5, 6, 10, 12, 13, 17, 20, 21, 23, 24 American Foundation for the Blind; p. 7, 15 Judith Lawton/Harcourt Education Ltd.; p. 11 Science Photo Library/Library of Congress; p. 16 Ronald Grant Archive; p. 25 Science Photo Library; p. 27 The Callahan Museum of the American Printing House for the Blind; Page icons Harcourt Education Ltd.

Cover photograph of Helen Keller, reproduced with permission of Getty Images/Hulton Archive.

Photo research by Melissa Allison and Fiona Orbell

Special thanks to Rebecca Vickers for her comments in the preparation of this book.

Every effort has been made to contact copyright holders of any material reproduced in this book. Any omissions will be rectified in subsequent printings if notice is given to the Publisher.

Contents

Some words are shown in bold, **like this**. You can find out what they mean by looking in the glossary.

Who Was Helen Keller?

Helen Keller had a childhood illness that left her unable to see or hear. She had to learn to live as a **deaf** and **blind** person.

Being deaf and blind made Helen's young life very hard.

Helen then spent her life helping other deaf-blind people. She worked hard for a better life and treatment for them. Her work helped many people.

Helen helped us to understand more about deaf and blind people.

Childhood Illness

Helen Keller was born on June 27, 1880. Her family lived in Tuscumbia, Alabama. When Helen was born, she could see and hear.

Helen's parents were Kate Adams Keller and Captain Arthur Keller.

Helen's illness may have been **meningitis**.

Helen became very ill in February 1882. She was only nineteen months old. Helen got better, but she was now **deaf** and **blind**. She would never learn to talk.

Growing up Wild

As Helen grew up, she was wild and hard to live with. She could not see, hear, or speak. She did not understand the world around her.

Helen was angry. She could not talk to other people or understand them. Her relatives thought she should be put in an **asylum**. Her mother said no.

Helen would scream and smash things.

Alexander Graham Bell

When Helen was six years old, her parents went to see a special doctor. He told them that Helen would never see or hear again.

Helen's parents wanted to make her life better.

The doctor told the family to speak to Alexander Graham Bell. He was famous because he had **invented** the telephone. Now he wanted to help **deaf** children.

Bell knew about deaf people because his mother and wife were deaf.

A Teacher for Helen

Alexander Graham Bell helped the Kellers find a teacher for Helen. Her name was Anne Mansfield Sullivan. Anne had once been nearly **blind** herself.

Anne Mansfield Sullivan became Helen's teacher.

Anne had **operations** to help her see. She still could not see very well. It was hard for her to find work. In March 1887, Anne Sullivan became Helen's teacher.

Anne came to live with Helen and her family at this house in Tuscumbia, Alabama.

A New Friendship

Anne taught Helen how to spell words with her fingers. She gave Helen a doll and wrote "d-o-l-l" with her finger into Helen's hand. Then she tried "c-a-k-e."

Helen learned to spell words, but she did not understand them.

Anne also tried to make Helen behave better. After a while, Helen became less wild. She stopped having temper tantrums.

Helen and Anne became close friends.

A Miracle!

On April 5, 1887, Anne put Helen's hand in water. She spelled "w-a-t-e-r" on Helen's other hand. Suddenly Helen understood. The cool running liquid had a name—it was called water!

This picture is from the movie *The Miracle Worker*. It shows the moment that the **miracle** happened.

Now Helen wanted to know the words for everything she touched.

Helen wanted Anne to teach her more and more words. Within a few hours, she knew 30 words!

So Much to Learn

Anne taught Helen how to read **Braille**. This is a special writing for **blind** people. You read Braille with your fingers, by feeling raised dots on the page.

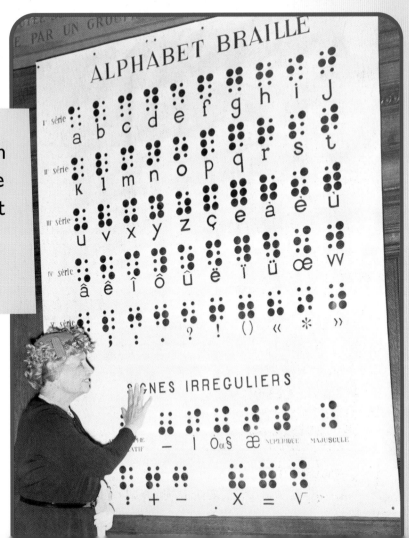

This is Helen when she was older. She is standing in front of the Braille alphabet.

Helen learned more than anyone thought was possible. She was the first **deaf-blind** person to get a college **degree**. Helen and Anne became famous.

Helen was given her degree on June 28, 1904.

Touring the World

Helen and Anne went on **lecture** tours.
They spoke to people about Helen's life.
Helen answered people's questions.
Anne **translated** every sentence.

Helen spent the next 50 years on lecture tours! This is a brochure from one of her lectures.

The First Appearance on the Lecture Platform of

HELEN KELLER

And her Teacher Mrs. Macy (Anne M. Sullivan)

SUBJECT

"The Heart and the Hand," or the Right Use of our Senses

Under the exclusive Management of
J. B. POND LYCEUM BUREAU
Metropolitan Life Building
New York City

Helen gave lectures all over the world.

In 1918 Helen began to work for **charities**. She wanted to make life better for **blind** people. At that time blind people had little education and often lived in **asylums**.

A Long and Busy Life

Anne Sullivan died on October 20, 1936. Helen continued to work around the world. She became ill in 1961 and stopped her tours and **lectures**.

Helen was still writing and reading when she was 80 years old.

In 1964, President Lyndon Johnson gave Helen a special medal for her work. Helen Keller died on June 1, 1968, when she was 87 years old.

Helen was given The Presidential Medal of Freedom for her work with **deaf-blind** people.

Why Is Helen Famous?

Helen Keller helped us understand the needs of **deaf** and **blind** people. She showed the world that deaf-blind people can do great things.

Helen told U.S. President John F. Kennedy about her work.

Today, there are machines that would have changed Helen's young life. Helen Keller's work helped to bring about the **invention** of these machines.

This **Braille** machine helps blind people read the writing on a computer screen.

More About Helen

We can find out more about Helen Keller from the American Foundation for the **Blind**. There are photos of Helen and **artifacts** from her life and **lecture** tours.

Helen wrote a book about her life in 1902.

HELEN KELLER

THE
STORY OF MY LIFE

Affectionately yours
Helen Keller

[Photo: Marshall]

HODDER AND STOUGHTON
ST. PAUL'S HOUSE, LONDON, E.C.4

There are websites and books about Helen's life. There is even a movie about Helen and Anne, called *The Miracle Worker*. Helen's childhood home is now a **museum**.

This special plaque was made for Helen in 1907. Helen liked it so much that she wrote her name on it.

Fact File

- The American Foundation for the **Blind** (AFB) helps people who are blind or have vision problems in the United States.

- Louis Braille (1809-1852) invented **Braille** writing. He lost his own sight when he was young. He spent his life helping blind people.

- Helen Keller Day is celebrated in the United States on June 27 every year.

- All her life, Helen wanted to talk. When she was a teenager, she went to the Wright-Humason School for the **Deaf**. She learned how to make a few sounds. Only the people who knew her well could understand them.

Timeline

1880   Helen Keller is born on June 27

1882   Helen Keller loses her sight and hearing

1886   The Kellers meet Alexander Graham Bell

1887   Anne Sullivan becomes Helen's teacher on March 3

1887   On April 5, Helen begins to understand that everything has a name

1900   Helen goes to Radcliffe College

1902   Helen writes *The Story of My Life*

1913   Helen and Anne start their **lecture** tours

1936   Anne dies on October 20

1955   Helen publishes a book about Anne Sullivan called *Teacher*

1961   Helen stops her lectures and tours

1968   Helen dies on June 1

Glossary

artifact something from long ago that we can still look at today

asylum hospital for people who were blind, deaf, or mentally ill

blind not able to see

Braille special writing for blind people, made up of raised dots that are read by touch

charity organization that helps people in need

deaf not able to hear

degree award you are given when you graduate from college

disability something that takes away a person's power or strength and makes it harder for them to do things

invent to think of and make something for the first time

lecture speech given by someone where an audience comes to listen

meningitis very serious illness that affects the brain

miracle something amazing that no one could have believed might happen

museum building where pieces of art or items of history are kept

operation work that a doctor does in a hospital to make a part of the body get better

translate explain so that someone can understand

More Books to Read

Adams, Colleen. *The Courage of Helen Keller.* New York, NY: The Rosen Publishing Group Inc., 2003.

Hurwitz, Johanna. *Helen Keller: Courage in The Dark.* New York, NY: Random House Inc., 2003.

Thompson, Gare. *Who Was Helen Keller?* Minneapolis, MN: Sagebrush Education Resources, 2003.

Places to Visit

You can visit Helen Keller's grave at:
Washington National Cathedral, Massachusetts and Wisconsin Aves NW, Washington, DC
(202) 537 6207

Index